GAINED A DAUGHTER BUT NEARLY LOST MY MIND:

How I Planned a Backyard Wedding During a Pandemic

by

Marlene Kern Fischer

TELEMACHUS PRESS

This book is a work of non-fiction. The events and characters are real. Believe me, you can't make this stuff up.

Gained a Daughter But Nearly Lost My Mind: How I Planned a Backyard Wedding During a Pandemic

Copyright © 2020 by Marlene Kern Fischer. All rights reserved, including the right to reproduce this book, or portions thereof, in any form. No part of this text may be reproduced, transmitted, downloaded, decompiled, reverse engineered, or stored in or introduced into any information storage and retrieval system, in any form or by any means, whether electronic or mechanical without the express written permission of the author. The scanning, uploading, and distribution of this book via the Internet or via any other means without the permission of the publisher is illegal and punishable by law. Please purchase only authorized editions and do not participate in or encourage electronic piracy of copyrighted materials.

The publisher does not have any control over and does not assume any responsibility for author or third-party websites or their content.

COVER ART AND DESIGN BY DANIELLE CLEMONS

Photographs used with permission

Published by Telemachus Press, LLC
7652 Sawmill Road, Suite 304
Dublin, Ohio 43017
http://www.telemachuspress.com

ISBN: 978-1-951744-42-7 (eBook)
ISBN: 978-1-951744-43-4 (Paperback)

FAMILY & RELATIONSHIPS / Marriage & Long-Term Relationships

Version 2020.09.15

TABLE OF CONTENTS

Acknowledgements i
Dedication iii
Foreword iv

February 2013 – April 2019:
    The Girlfriend/The Engagement 1
The Planning Phase 5
Wedding Dress Shopping
    With the Bride 7
Love in the Time of Corona 13
Unwinding the Wedding 19
From Lemons to Lemonade 23
The Weather 27
My Dress 31
The Battle Royale 35
Where to Stay 41
Hide and Seek 45
Almost There 47
Sharing a Bathroom 49
Tradition! 53
The Wedding 59
Phish 71
Going the Extra 2,999 Miles 79

Phish Timeline 83
What is My Daughter-in-law Going to
    Call Me? 87
Advice to the Newlyweds 91
Losing My Mind 95
Who Will Play Me in the
    Motion Picture? 99
Wrapping it Up 103

About the Author 109

ACKNOWLEDGEMENTS

I'd like to thank Eric and Danielle for falling in love, deciding to get married and sticking with their original wedding date, despite everything. Your love for each other is truly an inspiration.

I'd like to thank my husband Mark who is always supportive and has encouraged my writing from the beginning. You had me at "Hello" 39 years ago as I entered Cable dormitory at Brandeis.

I'd like to thank my other kids, Jonah and Isaac, who read, like and share almost everything I write. Plus, they were super patient during the wedding planning. You are amazing sons and brothers.

Thank you to my extended family, new and old, who helped us pull off this pandemic wedding.

Special shout-out to my friend, editor and Essay Moms partner, Helene Hirsch Wingens. You make everything I write sound better. Plus, you know all my stories.

Thank you to my friend and beta reader Sara Podrasky. You did an awesome job and I really appreciate your help.

Thank you to all my readers on *Thoughts From Aisle 4*; you have helped me create an amazing tribe and I am grateful for each and every one of you.

DEDICATION

This book is for everyone who likes a good story as well as anyone who has had to plan a wedding during this crazy time.

FOREWORD

I didn't set out to write a book. It's not like I woke up one morning and thought "I've organized all my closets during this pandemic and I have some free time on my hands so I think I'd like to write a book."

Many of the posts in *Gained a Daughter But Almost Lost My Mind* originally appeared on my Facebook page, *Thoughts From Aisle 4*. I noticed that my columns about the wedding did really well; my readers seemed to appreciate what my family was going through. And when I was in town, people would stop me to tell me how much they enjoyed hearing about the wedding plans and then the wedding itself. I am still getting the nicest comments and well wishes.

I realized that people love, love. And they love to laugh. Especially these days. This was a story that was both sweet and funny. So, I decided to edit and add to the original posts and compile them into a book. I figured that, at the very least, it would be a nice legacy to leave my not-yet-born grandchildren.

What you are about to read is a collection of vignettes about a wedding that happened despite a small thing like a global pandemic. It's a tribute to my family and the very true story of my experience.

I hope you enjoy,

XO
Marlene

GAINED A DAUGHTER BUT NEARLY LOST MY MIND:

How I Planned a Backyard Wedding During a Pandemic

"When you realize you want to spend the rest of your life with somebody, you want the rest of your life to start as soon as possible."

—When Harry Met Sally

FEBRUARY 2013 – APRIL 2019
THE GIRLFRIEND/THE ENGAGEMENT

We met her the weekend of our son's college graduation. Although they had only been together a few months, we already knew she was special to him. She sat with us during commencement and a few people asked if she was our daughter because she has similar coloring to our youngest son.

Fast forward six years ...

My son proposed to his girlfriend and she said "yes!" Although she had felt like family for a long time and it was almost a foregone conclusion that they would get married, it was still nice when it became official.

I had made no secret of the fact that I really liked her, and I thought that they were a perfect fit. Plus, I was finally going to have a daughter!

The proposal was incredibly romantic. Since they met at Washington University in St. Louis, my son flew out there early in the morning and left a plane ticket for her for later in the day with a note which basically said, "Meet me in St. Louis." I had helped him choose an engagement ring weeks earlier.

He asked her to marry him on their former college campus. We were able to watch as it was live streamed from a friend's phone—the wonders of modern technology. I cried.

Thus began the whole wedding planning phase.

Down on one knee in St. Louis

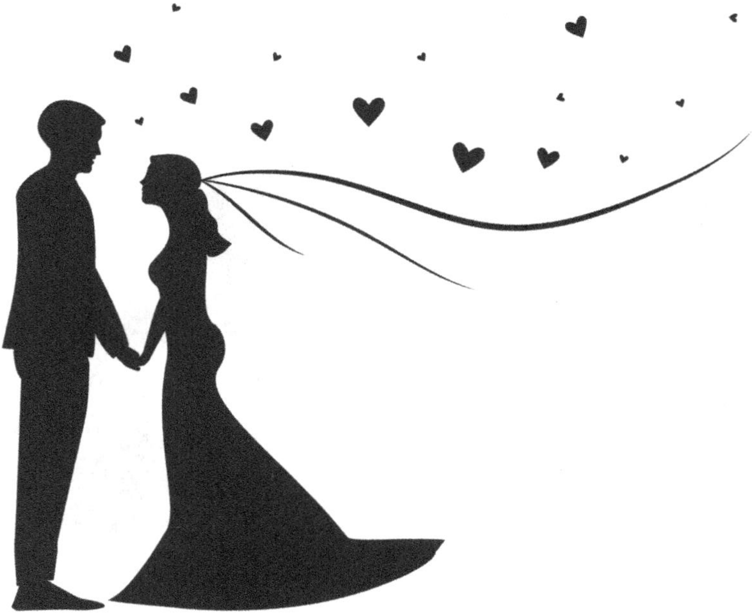

THE PLANNING PHASE

*I*mmediately after their engagement, we jumped into planning the wedding. My husband and I have been married for 33 years and I had forgotten how much angst goes into figuring out all the little and big things that make up a perfect wedding.

Being mom of the groom and not mom of the bride, I suspected that mine would be more of a walk-on role. I was happy to listen, give financial and emotional support and offer advice when needed, which I imagined wouldn't be all that often.

My son wanted a New Year's Eve wedding in New York. My almost daughter wanted a summer wedding in D.C. They looked at venues in both places and decided D.C. made the most sense. There wasn't enough time to plan a wedding for December 31, so they chose Thursday, July 2, 2020 as their wedding date. They figured a holiday weekend would make it easier for friends and family to travel.

There were so many details to work through. They ended up booking a wharf for the ceremony and a nearby hotel for the party. Flowers, invitations (which never ended up going to print), the band, photographer and restaurant for the rehearsal dinner were all chosen. The guest list was carefully and painstakingly curated. Things were starting to fall into place. I schlepped into Manhattan to have a dress custom made for myself, meeting with a designer a good friend had recommended.

But what was really important was the bride's dress . . .

WEDDING DRESS SHOPPING WITH THE BRIDE

I've always loved the show *Say Yes to the Dress* because in a house full of males (I have three sons), it was crucial to find ways to stay in touch with my girly side. That show fit the bill. So, when my son's fiancée invited me to go wedding dress shopping with her, her sister, mom and aunt, I was delighted, excited and honored.

I admit I was also a little nervous about the whole thing. I wasn't sure what to wear—I'm usually pretty casual but I didn't think my frayed jean shorts would do, so I opted for my tried and true white jeans and a crisp tie dye t-shirt. My husband pointed out that my t-shirt had a tear near the collar, but I explained that it was supposed to be there, and I had paid a lot for that tear. It added to my not-trying-too-hard-but-still-chic vibe.

I was a little concerned about offering too many opinions on this very important shopping expedition, so I decided I would just smile and nod a lot. I even practiced in the mirror. My daughter-in-law is beautiful with a figure to die for, making it impossible for her to look bad in anything. Even so, I didn't want to overstep my bounds.

I had done some research, so I would be knowledgeable about bridal couture. Back 33 years ago when I worked in public relations for a department store, I actually wrote a press release about new trends in wedding gowns.

Suffice it to say that a lot has changed since then. My grandmother would be appalled to know that maternity wedding gowns are now a thing. Poofy sleeves are out, and mermaid styles are in.

Giddy with anticipation I headed into the city and we met up at the first store. As predicted, my son's bride looked stunning in everything. I actually commented on how her figure matched the figure of the mannequin displaying a gown.

I kept my vow and expressed my thoughts when called upon, but only then and without being pushy. She tried on several dresses and then we went to a second store where we had another appointment. When the salesperson asked us to identify ourselves, my son's future mother-in-law introduced me as Mom 2, which I just loved. I wondered if perhaps the salesperson was confused and thought that me and Mom 1 were a couple but hey, who cares? I feel that the term mother-in-law may be as displeasing as poofy sleeves and am more than happy to replace it with Mom 2.

After the first two stores, we took a break for lunch at the Plaza. I felt just like Eloise. All this girl time was starting to spoil me.

Although no dress was actually chosen that day, there were a few leading contenders.

My son's fiancée wanted to think about the dresses she saw, and possibly consider some others. I liked how mindful she was about this decision; mindfulness kind of defines who she is.

To make sure I wasn't getting too used to female conversation and companionship, I called my son on the phone after I left our little shopping group. Our dialogue was brief and completely unsatisfying, although I did learn he was eating ramen noodles. I was back in my element.

In the end, I was glad to have had the chance to go wedding dress shopping with a daughter.

Gained a Daughter But Nearly Lost My Mind

The bride in the dress she said "yes" to

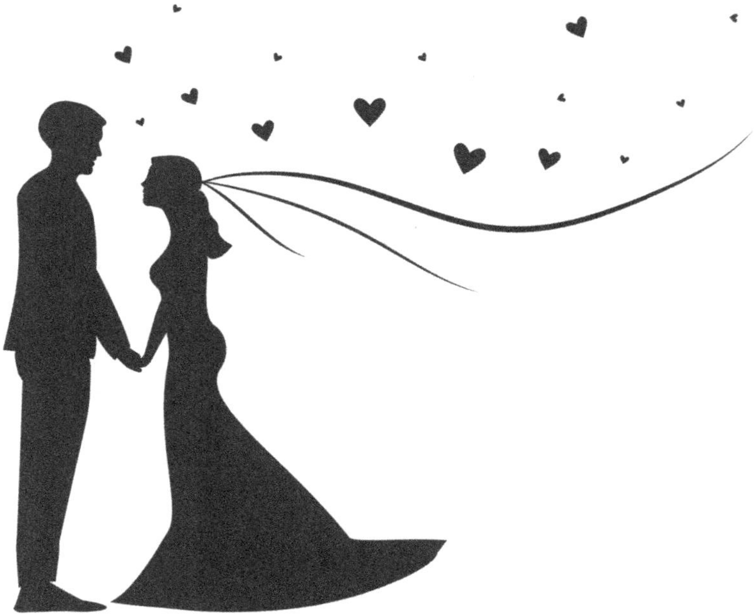

LOVE IN THE TIME OF CORONA

As I mentioned in The Planning Phase, the wedding was set to take place on July 2nd, in Washington D.C. By the time March 2020 rolled in, everything was pretty much done. All that was left was to send out the invitations. My talented almost daughter had designed the invitations herself, but they hadn't gone to print yet which was fortunate, because March 2020 was about to throw us (and the entire planet) some serious curveballs.

In mid-March, the world basically came to a screeching halt. We initially thought that we would be fine by July. Looking back, I realize that we were in denial and/or somewhat delusional. As the pandemic dragged on, we understood that it would not be possible or safe to have a wedding in July.

We entered the "What should we do now?" phase.

The kids considered getting married in the fall. However, my son (who by the way told me to stock my pantry months earlier in anticipation of the virus and quarantining) thought there might be a second wave. They didn't want to be in a position where they would have to cancel again.

They looked into having the wedding on another date further into the future—including the following summer. On the bright side, I figured that if they waited until summer 2021 to get married, I would have some time to lose the corona weight I had gained.

They thought about having a civil ceremony so at least they would be legally married. Or a small religious ceremony in a park somewhere or their rooftop in Brooklyn with just the immediate family, a *chuppah* (wedding canopy) and a rabbi. There were lots of possibilities. Every day my son and daughter seemed to change their minds about what they wanted to do. Some days they wanted to talk about it and other days they didn't. It became a touchy subject.

My son's bachelor party and my almost daughter's bridal shower were the first wedding related events to be officially cancelled.

Things were not looking good.

I have to say that, for the most part, they were very adult about the whole thing. A wedding is a pretty major life event and they didn't whine at all. Or much. In a text to me, my almost daughter said, "None of this is ideal and it's very disappointing (I've made my peace with it), but if the worst thing that happens to all of us during coronavirus is that our wedding is moved, then we are all blessed!" I admired her attitude.

Remarkably, the uncertainty did not seem to affect their relationship. In fact, they seemed more solid than ever. And that was really what was important. I could see that they understood that what mattered most was not when or how they would get married, but that they would figure it out and get through it together. A little thing like a pandemic was no match for their love.

It was a beautiful thing to behold.

The invitation which never made it to print

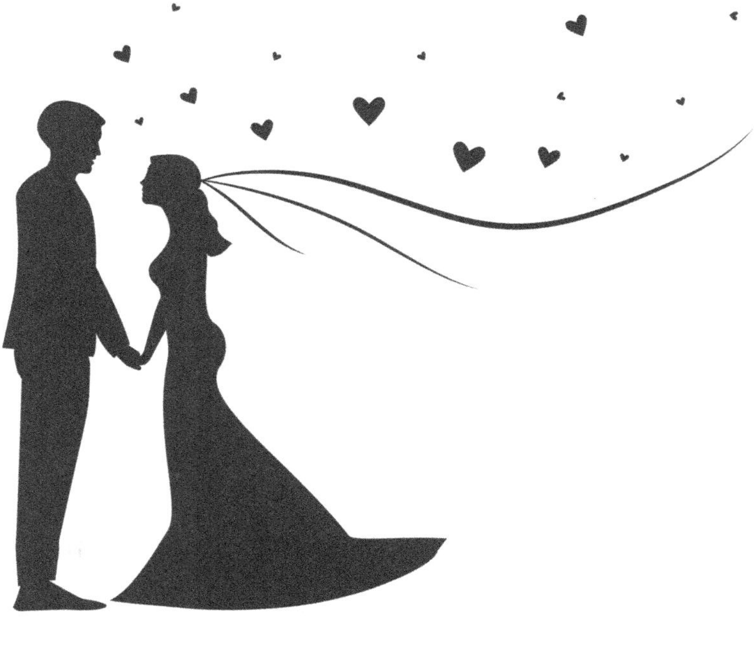

UNWINDING THE WEDDING

Turns out that trying to unwind a wedding is an even bigger headache than planning one in the first place. Once it became clear that it couldn't happen, some of the vendors, but not all, agreed to return our deposits.

I had paid for my custom dress in full, but my dress designer didn't want to return any of my money, even though I hadn't gone for a single fitting and he hadn't done any work. We ultimately came to an agreement but not before my blood pressure had been raised to a dangerous level and my sanity severely challenged.

My son and almost daughter decided that they still wanted to get married on their original date. As per Jewish custom, you aren't really supposed to cancel a wedding. I was totally on board with their decision.

With our options severely limited, we decided to have the wedding in my backyard, and I was cast as the wedding planner. My only qualifications for the role were the three bar mitzvahs I had planned for my sons, years earlier. I hired someone local to help me with the flowers and table rental. I wanted my almost daughter and son to have a special day despite everything.

I couldn't see doing it half-heartedly; I wanted to go all out. Or as all out as you can go during a global pandemic.

The new guest list was small. It shrank from over 200 to just the immediate family who would have to sit socially distanced at two farmhouse tables. The theme was do-it-yourself rustic. And love.

I discovered that even a micro wedding was difficult to plan during this time and presented many challenges. The bride's family would have to drive up from Maryland. My mother and my mother-in-law were trapped in Florida. We had to make sure that everyone in attendance had been quarantining.

The weather became a factor and I started looking into buying or renting a tent in case of rain. But I was really hoping for a nice day.

My almost daughter and I did a walk-through of the "venue" (aka my backyard). We discussed where the *chuppah* and tables would be set up, where they would sign their *ketubah* (marriage contract) and who the witnesses would be.

The hope was that in summer 2021 my son and daughter would be able to celebrate with their friends. We took to calling the cancelled wedding "Wedding 0," the backyard wedding "Wedding 1" and the future celebration "Wedding 2." That way, we didn't get confused when we discussed the many weddings.

I told my younger sons that if and when they decide to marry, they should consider eloping. But I didn't really mean it.

Because I knew that once I saw my son and almost daughter under the *chuppah* it would all be worth it. I wanted it to be perfect because I love my kids. Plus I'm a romantic at heart.

FROM LEMONS TO LEMONADE

My son ended up having his bachelor party after all. Via Zoom of course. My youngest son and almost daughter picked up the champagne his friends had ordered for him at a nearby liquor store.

I don't know what went on during the party other than it went on for hours and people dressed up like members of the band Phish—my son's favorite band. His actual bachelor party was supposed to be in Atlanta where one of the band members was to have performed.

While the party was going on, my almost daughter came over (at that point she and my son were staying in my snowbird mom's empty house nearby) and we discussed their reimagined wedding. Other than the date, everything about the wedding was going to be different. Among other things, we talked about her wedding bouquet, and whether her dress was going to be ready and if it wasn't, what would she wear?

The morning after the bachelor party, my youngest son reported back that it was a success. I didn't ask for too many details other than who was "there" because I've seen enough movies to know that what happens at the bachelor party stays at the bachelor party. I was glad my son was able to have a party, even if it was a virtual one and not the weekend away and celebration he had hoped for.

Meanwhile, the wedding plans kept changing and then changing again.

The saying goes, "When life gives you lemons, make lemonade." Definitely words to live by. The coronavirus may have taken some things away from my son and almost daughter, but not the most important things. I was so proud of them for forging ahead with love, flexibility, pragmatism and hope. I think that the way they handled things bodes well for their future as a married couple.

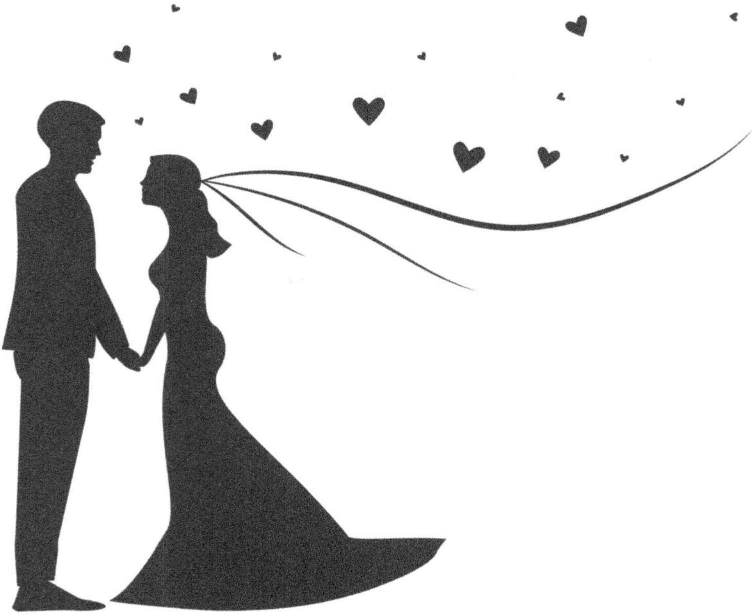

THE WEATHER

Outdoor parties are not for the faint of heart. But sometimes you just don't have a choice.

July weather can be tricky. It can be a thousand degrees. Or even worse, raining. Or even worse than that, there can be a tropical storm or hurricane with a NAME. Named storms can be very scary.

As soon as we were 14 days out, I started checking all the weather apps to see what July 2nd would be like. My husband thought this was odd behavior, saying "It will be what it will be. Why worry?" How delightful for him.

If I could live in his world for ten minutes, I'd probably be a much happier and better adjusted person.

A rain date was not an option. And a tent would only work if there weren't heavy downpours. Not to mention the fact that we are a pretty nervous group; we all run for cover at the first clap of thunder.

We decided to rent the clubhouse in our development as plan B or C (at this point I had lost track of what letter we were up to) but it was not an ideal backup plan. My son said he wasn't too keen on getting married in the same place where he had his ninth birthday party but if the weather didn't cooperate, there would be no choice. I could only promise him that there would be no piñata at this party.

As the date got closer, both my almost daughter and I kept checking weather apps. It's noteworthy that the various apps tend to disagree on the forecast; one might say 60% possibility of precipitation (POP) while another might have the POP at 10%.

We wanted to believe whichever app had the better forecast. However, we remained fully aware that until the day of the wedding, none of them were likely to be all that accurate.

Knowing that weather forecasting is often more art than science didn't stop me from looking. And obsessing. I couldn't help myself. Which is why, up until Wedding 1, I had avoided outdoor parties since my kids were little.

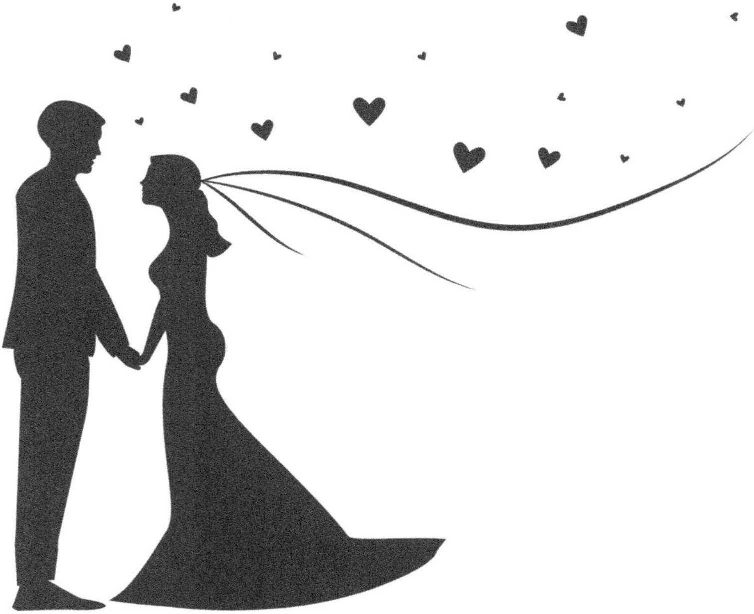

MY DRESS

For the three or four months before the wedding I had worn the pandemic uniform, stretchy pants and a beat up t-shirt. The key word here is stretchy.

I was fortunate enough to find a super cute dress online which screamed "backyard wedding." But I was going to need some serious shapewear; it was just the harsh truth. Enter Spanx.

Some of you may be thinking to yourselves "Why not be comfortable? Forget the undergarments which constrict all your internal organs." But I would not do that for several reasons.

To start with, there was going to be a photographer present. For the same reason I held my breath for an hour in a hair salon to correct my do-it-yourself hair color, I wanted to look my best. My standards might have been a little low at that point, but they still existed. I had a single remaining shred of pride.

My almost daughter is super thin. And so are her mom and sister. These are people who exercise and run for FUN. Word has it that before they eat their turkey on Thanksgiving, they all go on a run. In my house before we eat the Thanksgiving meal, we watch the Macy's Parade. While eating breakfast. Don't get me wrong, I really like my *machatunim* (Yiddish for almost daughter's parents). They are super great, if not a little too active.

Back when there were supposed to be 200 plus guests at the wedding, I figured I could stand with people who looked more like me weight-wise and blend in. But now that we were having a micro wedding it was basically going to be just me and them. Nowhere to hide. So, Spanx it was.

I was afraid that after so many months of letting it all hang out, my body would go into some sort of shock when forced into tight undergarments. Like it might reject the Spanx. This was a real concern. I wondered if anyone had ever burst through Spanx.

In addition, I bought a pair of chunky heel shoes so I wouldn't puncture our lawn with every step or get stuck in the grass. I found the shoes at a consignment shop in my town. I stood in an alley to try them on and felt like Cinderella when they fit. They had little horses on the buckles. And the dress I bought had horses on it too. I felt that it was definitely a sign, although I'm not sure of what.

I was wearing slippers a lot while in quarantine. And flip flops. I knew that my new over two-inch heels were going to feel like stilts.

The bottom line was that I might not feel all that comfortable as I watched my son and almost daughter exchange vows. But I would do my best to look as good as I could.

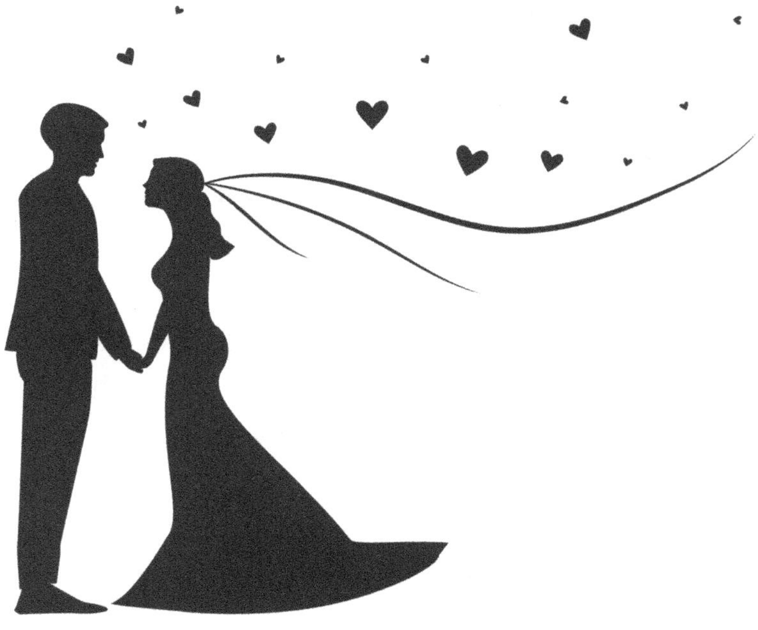

THE BATTLE ROYALE

We had a battle going on at my house. More specifically, outside my house. It was my husband vs. the woodland creatures.

My husband had wisely left all the wedding details to me, save one: the garden. He decided to use this opportunity to beautify our yard in advance of the kids' BIG DAY.

He bought flowers and planted them in the front beds. And the back beds, amongst the rocks. And it was good. But it wasn't good enough. So, I went with him to the nursery and bought more flowers to keep the other flowers company. I was happy to go because it wasn't like I was getting out much.

And then he planted those flowers as well. Since our yard backs on the woods, creatures like deer and rabbits like to nibble on our flowers. To combat this danger, he bought deer repellant. Which sort of smells like a combination of urine and vomit.

Every few days my husband, bless his heart, went outside and sprayed all the flowers. And then we all headed inside and closed all the windows because it smelled that bad. Good luck to any animal who wanted to eat our flowers after my husband had sprayed; all I can say is that they would have had to be really hungry.

Then my husband went back to the nursery a third time and purchased bushes. And he hired people to plant all those bushes because it was too big of a project for him to tackle alone.

He also planted his annual vegetable and herb garden and put a higher fence around it to keep critters from enjoying our basil and lettuce. I do enjoy the produce we pick from the garden; we've got a real farm to table thing going on. Nothing tastes better to my husband than food he grew with his own hands.

Did I mention the tiki torches? My husband felt we needed tiki torches to keep the bugs away. We were now the proud owners of about twenty tiki torches which he strategically placed around our backyard.

I have to give credit where credit is due. He transformed our backyard into a tropical paradise. I sort of felt like I was in Hawaii except then I remembered I was in my backyard during a pandemic and not Hawaii.

I really hoped that he would win his war against nature. Because if he didn't, I feared it would break him.

Cute but a threat to our flowers

A man and his tiki torches

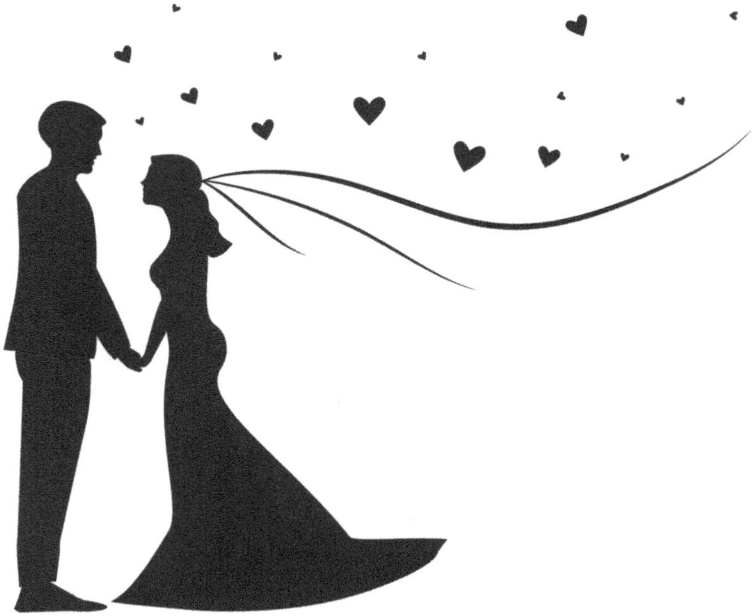

WHERE TO STAY

My almost daughter's parents had concerns about where to stay. They were coming from Maryland and the trip to New York was too long to do back and forth in a day.

The mom didn't want to stay in a hotel and I totally got that. Although the number of Covid-19 cases around here were declining, hotels were still risky. My house wasn't really an option either; every nook and cranny was filled because all my kids were home. Plus, I think they weren't comfortable staying in my house for the same reasons they didn't want to go to a hotel.

In a moment of genius my almost daughter's dad suggested they rent an RV. Now, just so you know, I've always had a dream of renting an RV and driving across the country.

Although the dad may have been joking when he initially suggested the RV, pretty soon we all realized what a terrific idea it was.

He called around and found a place that could deliver a small RV to our driveway. It had a bathroom and running water; all we had to do was plug it into the outlet in our garage. My husband has an electric car, so we actually have a high voltage outlet. We hoped the RV wouldn't blow a fuse or anything. We measured our driveway and the RV just fit. It was like it was meant to be.

Actually, sleeping in an RV sounded like it might be kind of fun. Plus, they would have a place to get dressed for the wedding. And how awesome was it that her parents would be able to just walk from our backyard to the front of our house when the party was over? No worries about drinking and driving.

What started out as an off-the-cuff suggestion, turned out to be the perfect solution.

The RV

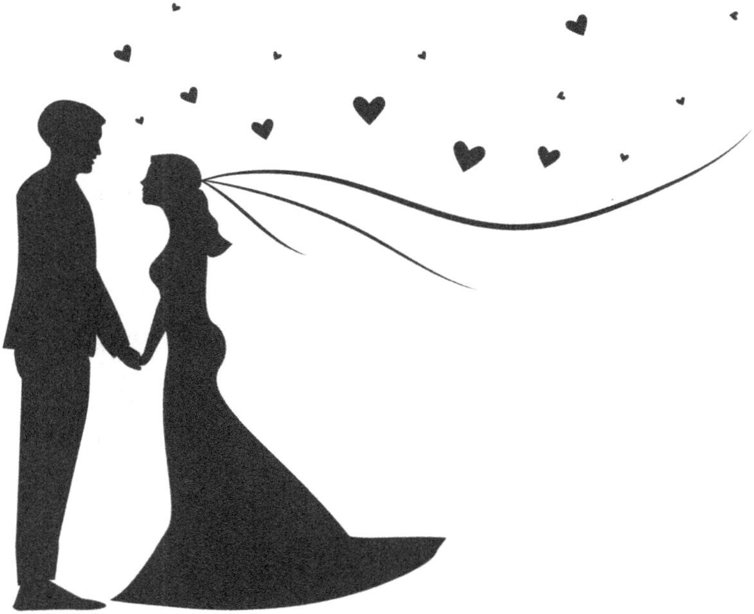

HIDE AND SEEK

My son decided he would observe the Jewish tradition in which the bride and groom don't see each other in the days leading up to the wedding.

It was a fine idea, except for the fact that they were both living here in this house which is regular size. I mean, it's a lot bigger than the two-bedroom, one-bathroom house I grew up in in Brooklyn but it's not palatial by any stretch of the imagination.

There were six of us living here, in this regular size house. Which means it was never surprising to see another family member in the kitchen or on the stairs. No one said "fancy meeting you here" when they bumped into someone else. In fact, if you wanted to be alone you needed to lock yourself in your bedroom or take a walk. Not that I ever felt the need to be alone (eye roll).

So, you can see how trying to stay completely away from one person might have been problematic.

My son moved into the basement while his bride had the run of the rest of the house. When he wanted to come upstairs he texted or called her to let her know that he was changing his location. I saw them dashing about the house; watching two fully grown adults play hide and seek was somewhat amusing, if not a little strange.

After being together for seven years I guess it was kind of sweet that they wanted to do this.

While working in my bedroom, I heard my oldest son yell "coming up" as my youngest son announced that his almost sister was in the upstairs bathroom.

Yup, it was just another day in the life of a family quarantined together before a wedding.

ALMOST THERE

The week of my son and almost daughter's wedding had finally arrived. At T minus five days, it looked like all systems were go.

I knew it had to be a precise mission. I was hoping that everything would go smoothly because in the time of Covid-19, there was only the slightest margin for error. Fortunately for all, my OCD came in handy for this undertaking.

Planning the wedding became a labor of love. Because as much stress as there was in the process of getting the bride and groom to the *chuppah*, I have to say that there are few greater joys than seeing your child find their person.

I knew I would be missing friends and family who could not be present at the wedding. Although there is something to be said for an intimate wedding, there's also joy in having the people you love surround you when something so momentous occurs.

Because of this virus, people have had to be alone in sickness and in health, in birth and death, and in all those special moments which give life meaning. But this was how it had to be.

Although our friends and family couldn't be there, I felt their love and support. And for that I was and am deeply grateful.

SHARING A BATHROOM

We live in a four-bedroom house with two bathrooms upstairs; one for me and my husband and a hall bathroom for my kids.

Having to share a bathroom was never a big issue for my sons. With a five-year gap between each of my three boys, they were generally all on different schedules and therefore didn't need to use the bathroom at the same time. Plus, when they were in there, they didn't take too long. Yeah, sometimes one of them complained that they couldn't gain access, but overall, it worked.

However, they had never shared a bathroom with a girl. Before a wedding.

My almost daughter did not want to have her makeup professionally done during a pandemic. But she wanted to look like she had had it professionally done. So, she ordered makeup. A lot of makeup, which arrived in boxes from Sephora almost daily. She took online tutorials. And practiced in front of the mirror in the bathroom.

She informed my boys that she would need the bathroom between 12 and 3 the day of the wedding to get ready and that they should plan accordingly.

My youngest son, who is only 19 and does not have all that much experience with women, was especially confused. He asked me what in the world a person could possibly do in a bathroom for three hours. I chuckled.

But I have to say, my sons were extremely good sports about everything wedding related and the bathroom request was no exception. Without complaint, they complied with my soon-to-be daughter's request and made sure the bathroom was available to her, showering well before the noon deadline. They even joked about it later in their wedding toast.

My almost daughter's makeup was flawless. No professional could have done a better job and she looked exquisite. If she ever decides to quit her job as a web designer she could have a career as a makeup artist.

After the happy couple packed up and departed for their honeymoon, my youngest son commented that, devoid of her makeup products, their bathroom looked so empty and big. I think it was good for him to have a taste of what it was like to share a bathroom with a female; the knowledge may come in handy for him at some point in the future.

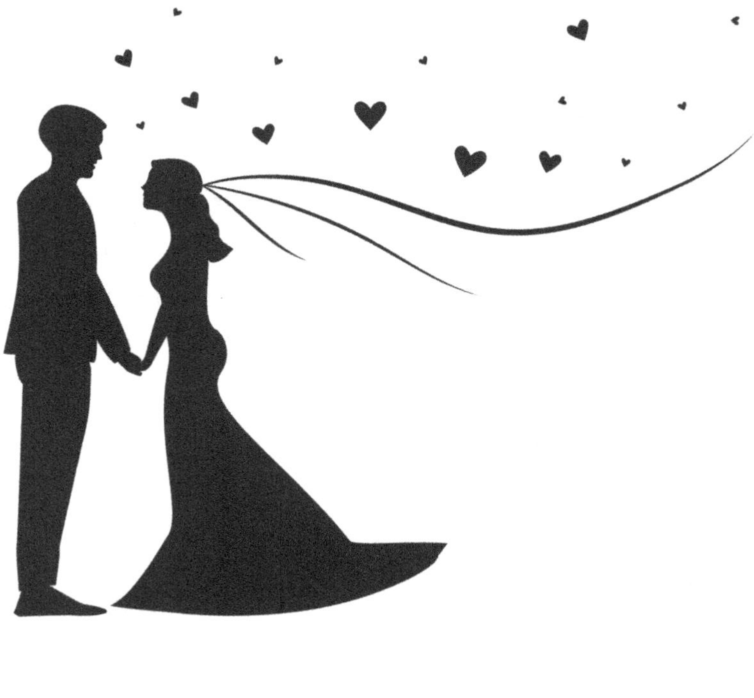

TRADITION!

There are a lot of traditions and symbolism in a Jewish wedding ceremony. After the bride and groom exchange rings and their formal vows, a glass wrapped in a cloth is placed at the groom's feet. He then smashes the glass after which everyone shouts "*Mazel tov!*" (congratulations). There are many explanations for this tradition, including remembering the destruction of the Temples in Jerusalem and recognizing that marriage can be as fragile as glass.

Jews get married under a *chuppah*, which represents a Jewish home. A *chuppah* can be ornate or plain; the *chuppah* at my wedding was a simple garden trellis adorned with flowers. A common practice is to use four poles to which a *tallis*—a Jewish prayer shawl—is attached at the top to the four corners, creating the "roof." When a friend heard that we might be having a backyard wedding, she offered to lend us the four wooden poles that her son and daughter-in-law had used for their *chuppah*. The plan was for each parent to hold one pole to form the four walls of the house.

We decided to use my husband's late father's tallis for the roof of the *chuppah*; our son was only two and a half years old when my father-in-law died, but they had had a close bond. The night before the wedding, we got the four poles from the garage where they had been stored for several weeks and my three sons and husband put the tallis on top. As they stood there holding it, I got tears in my eyes. My baby was all grown up and about to be married. After all the planning, it was really happening.

My late father's prayer shawl was smaller and we decided it would be perfect to wrap the couple in during the ceremony as a symbol of their unification. The bride's great great grandfather's *kiddush* cup (a wine cup over which blessings are recited) was also used in the ceremony, as it had been at all her cousins' weddings. The cup had traveled with him from Poland to Mexico to Costa Rica to Cuba and, finally, to the U.S. Past generations were well-represented under that *chuppah* and we felt their presence. I know they would have approved wholeheartedly of the union and the keeping of the traditions.

Each of the four siblings of the bride and groom held a pole while my husband and I and my almost daughter's parents walked our children down the aisle. Once there, each parent replaced one of the siblings. The choreography allowed all of the immediate members to be near the couple, surrounding them with our love.

As I stood under the *chuppah* and listened to the couple exchange the most beautiful vows I've ever heard, I thought about my son as an intense little boy, and then a willful teen, when I worried about him being able to put someone else's needs before his own. When his voice broke while speaking to his bride of his devotion, I was close enough to put my hand on his shoulder for support. I hope my son and new daughter can always feel my hand on their shoulders, steadying them when they need it. Because I've learned that at some point we all need steadying.

A few weeks after the wedding, I returned the poles to my friend because they were going to loan them out to another bride and groom. I like to think of them as traveling poles, going from one couple to another to help them carry on this tradition, creating a *chuppah* and wedding that is meaningful and unique to them.

Gained a Daughter But Nearly Lost My Mind

My husband and sons with the chuppah the night before the wedding

"Love recognizes no barriers. It jumps hurdles, leaps fences, penetrates walls to arrive at its destination full of hope."

—Maya Angelou

THE WEDDING

*M*agic happened in my backyard.

Despite several days of rain which preceded the wedding day, the morning of the wedding we woke up to a clear blue sky.

Perhaps the beautiful weather was due to all the good vibes people sent our way (thank you).

Per Jewish tradition, my son fasted on his wedding day. He began the day reading Torah with a group of ten men (an assortment of family and neighbors) in our backyard. I give him extra points for trying to keep things traditional, especially during a pandemic.

The bride began getting ready with help from me, her sister and mom. She put flowers in her hair and borrowed a pair of pearl drop earrings from me.

The couple participated in the *bedeken* ceremony which is based on the biblical story of Jacob who labored for seven years for his bride of choice and was fooled into marrying her sister. Since that time all Jewish husbands check under the veil to make sure they are getting the right bride.

Then they had a *tisch* where the groom is supposed to speak words of wisdom from the Torah and is raucously interrupted with songs and shouts of well-wishes. Next the Rabbi read the ketubah (marriage contract) which explains the obligations of a Jewish husband.

It finally was showtime. With 14 members of the immediate families and a small number of socially distanced friends and family looking on, we walked our son down a makeshift aisle to the *chuppah*. Then he sat down at his keyboard to play his bride's favorite Phish song as her parents walked her down the aisle. The couple's vows touched everyone and we all cried. They said that they felt that they were able to share personal feelings and memories because the wedding was so intimate.

Although Covid-19 was the reason my always son and now daughter's wedding took place in my backyard instead of a big fancy venue, Covid-19 did not intrude (other than to keep our guests socially distanced). Reality left us alone for the day.

After a year of planning and then unplanning and then planning anew, we all learned a few things.

A wedding does not have to be big or fancy to be perfect.

The people you love will always manage to be present in some way or form. Although many of our friends and relatives could not be in attendance physically, they sent wishes via calls and cards and texts and funny videos.

One of my son's best friends, who lives in LA and had been the King of Quarantine, decided he couldn't bear not to be at the ceremony. So, he booked a very last-minute flight and showed up in time for the pre-wedding festivities. It was gestures like his as well as others, big and small, which made the day extraordinary.

People showed up to pray in the morning. Friends and neighbors drove by at a specified time to shower the couple, who sat on chairs on our front lawn, with good wishes. At our request, a fire truck from town joined the parade. My friend's son flew his drone overhead so that we could have aerial footage. It took a village and ours was exceptional. The food, cake, clothes, etc. came from merchants in our little town and we felt good about supporting local businesses.

My new daughter said that she had only been to big weddings and didn't know something small and simple could be so special.

And special it was. In addition to the intimate ceremony, the toasts were funny and sweet. The Phish cover band my son insisted on hiring played two sets like at a real show and was awesome. We all danced and ate and drank and had a blast. We lifted the bride and groom on chairs and did the *hora*, a traditional celebratory Jewish dance.

I'm not saying small weddings are better. I'm not saying big weddings are better. But I am saying that maybe this pandemic showed us that there is more than one way to do things.

The tables

The bride's sister helping her get ready

The bride and groom

Gained a Daughter But Nearly Lost My Mind

Walking our son to the marriage canopy

The ceremony

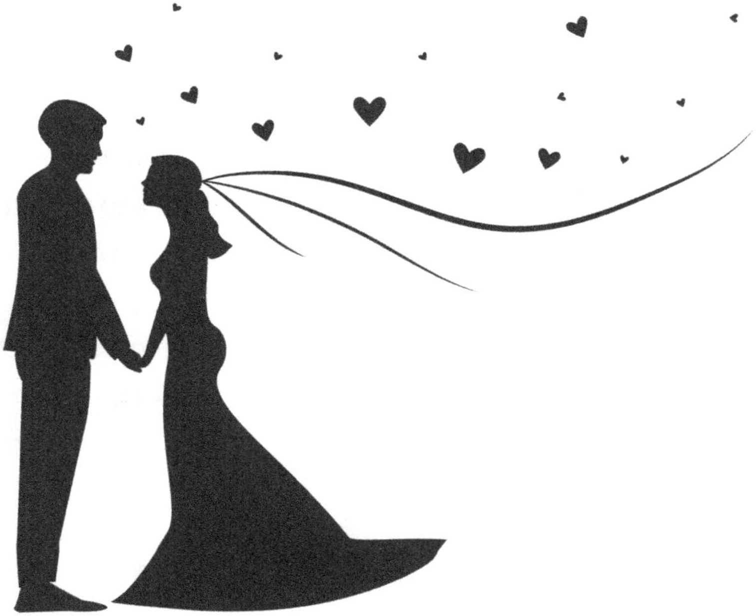

"I don't believe coincidences are chance events. I think they're the times we happened to see the mysterious pattern connecting everything."

—David French
Salt-Water Moons

PHISH

Exactly one year before the wedding, I met members of the band Phish while vacationing in Rhode Island. It was noteworthy because of my son's obsession with them. I'm not one to read into things but, looking back, I feel like it may have been a sign of things to come.

Right before the world changed, my son went to Mexico to see Phish perform. He went with my middle son, his then fiancée (now wife), her sister and husband, and his brother. It was a sibling bonding trip. My youngest son had no interest; he's not a phan.

While in Mexico, my son happened to meet a rabbi who happened to be from our town and really liked him. Small world, right? Apparently, my son even commented that if they weren't getting married in D.C. by his fiancée's rabbi, he would have wanted the Phish Rabbi, as we took to calling him, to perform the ceremony.

When the pandemic hit and we reimagined the wedding, it somehow became a Phish-themed wedding. The bride and groom contacted Phish Rabbi—Joshua Strom—and he said he'd be delighted to perform the ceremony.

I ordered a cake with my son and now daughter's wedding logo, which was a takeoff on the Phish logo. My son hired a Phish cover band called Uncle Ebenezer. The couple ordered Phish t-shirts for both families. I even got their wedding logo printed on face masks.

I felt like my one failure was the fact that I could not get any members of the real band to wish my kids congratulations. I came close when a friend of mine ran into Phish's bass guitarist Mike Gordon at her lake house in Vermont, but she only saw him the one time and didn't get a chance to ask him.

I reached out to Trey Anastasio, the band's lead singer, who I had met on vacation but I guess he was busy or didn't get the message, because if he had, I know he would have responded. He's that nice.

In any event, the bride and groom did their first dance on trampolines to a Phish song (of course) and when my son posted the video, he tagged Mike Gordon who he could see had viewed it. I think that was almost as good as getting a congratulatory message from them.

The cover band was fantastic and we all had so much fun dancing the night away. The happy couple now say they couldn't imagine their wedding any other way than how it all happened.

When I met Trey a year ago, I jokingly asked him if he would play at my son's wedding and he jokingly said "yes." And in a way he was there.

I have no idea what any of it meant. But I do think it meant something.

Gained a Daughter But Nearly Lost My Mind

Me and hubby and Trey

The wedding cake

Both families in our Phish t-shirts

"Friendship is the hardest thing in the world to explain. It's not something you learn in school. But if you haven't learned the meaning of friendship, you really haven't learned anything."

—Muhammad Ali

GOING THE EXTRA 2,999 MILES

There are stories within stories from my son and daughter-in-law's wedding. Layer upon layer of tales of how the day became such a success.

Here's one of the stories that stands out. It's a story of friendship.

The bride and groom, now husband and wife, are fortunate to have many amazing friends. Friends who showed up for them in various ways. And it's not really fair to single out any one person. But I will anyway.

My son has a particular friend who he met at the very beginning of college. They joined the same fraternity and became brothers in every sense.

This friend once spent some time visiting us and during his visit got the worst case of food poisoning I've ever been unfortunate enough to witness. While my son sat on our deck drinking beer with another friend, I tended to this young man, who threw up more times in a short period than I had ever seen. As the kids like to say, it was pretty epic.

In any event, that was over a decade ago and this now full adult has redeemed himself many times over.

Instead of just calling him "the friend" I will call him "Louis."

As I mentioned a few chapters ago, Louis lives in California. And we live in New York. Despite the fact that, right from the beginning, this young man had been adamant about quarantining, he could not bear to miss seeing his good friend get married.

So, in the wee hours of the morning before the wedding, Louis booked a flight to New York and got on it.

Let me explain that I am not a spontaneous person. I plan things out to a ridiculous degree, which causes me (and the people around me) to stress. So the thought of just deciding last minute to hop on a plane during a pandemic is mind blowing to me. Like how does this even work? You call the airport and say "Hello, I would like a ticket for an hour from now?" And then you pack a toothbrush and a clean pair of underwear (I hope) and leave your apartment?

Louis made it in time for the festivities. (And don't worry, he wore a mask and socially-distanced.) And the fact that he went that extra 2,999 miles meant everything to my son and new daughter.

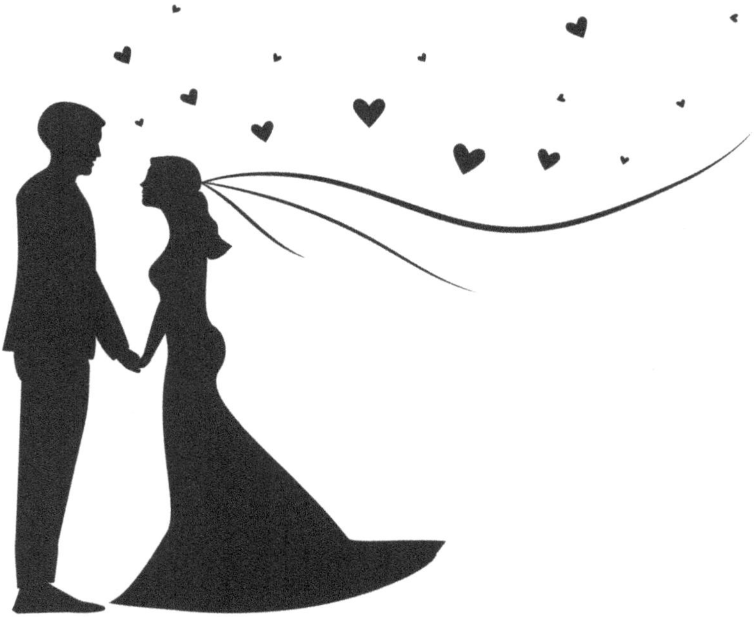

PHISH TIMELINE

June 2, 2009—Son goes to his first Phish show.

2009–2020—Son goes to many many Phish shows all over the country. I am confused. But, whatever.

July 8, 2019—I meet a guy in the cabana next to mine while on vacation in Rhode Island. I have no clue who he is but enjoy listening to him play the guitar and sing. Turns out to be Mike Gordon of Phish. Say what? Husband figures out the guy standing nearby on sand is Trey Anastasio. I go up to Trey and have a wonderful chat with him—Trey takes my phone and calls my son who is at work. Son's mind is blown. I earn the mom-of-the-year award.

December 2019—I go to my first Phish concert on Long Island. Am impressed. Phish plays *Avinu Malkeinu*, a Jewish prayer usually recited during the High Holidays. It gives me chills. Get offered weed. Politely decline. Get offered acid. Politely decline.

February 2020—Son and almost daughter meet a rabbi-who-happens-to-be-from-our-small-town at a Phish concert in Mexico.

March—Pandemic shuts down world. No more Phish concerts. Son is sad.

April—Son and almost daughter decide to cancel the big D.C. wedding set for July 2.

May—Son and almost daughter decide to have a backyard wedding with Phish Rabbi as officiant.

July 2—Phish themed wedding happens. Turns out magical. I have a new daughter. We dance the night away to Phish cover band.

July 21—Mike's mom Marjorie reads my Phish wedding story on my blog and writes to me to tell me she loves it. Says she will forward it to her son. Kids and Phish Rabbi are thrilled.

August 3—CONGRATULATIONS CARD ARRIVES FROM PHISH IN THE MAIL. I did it!

All is right in the universe.

Congratulations card from Phish

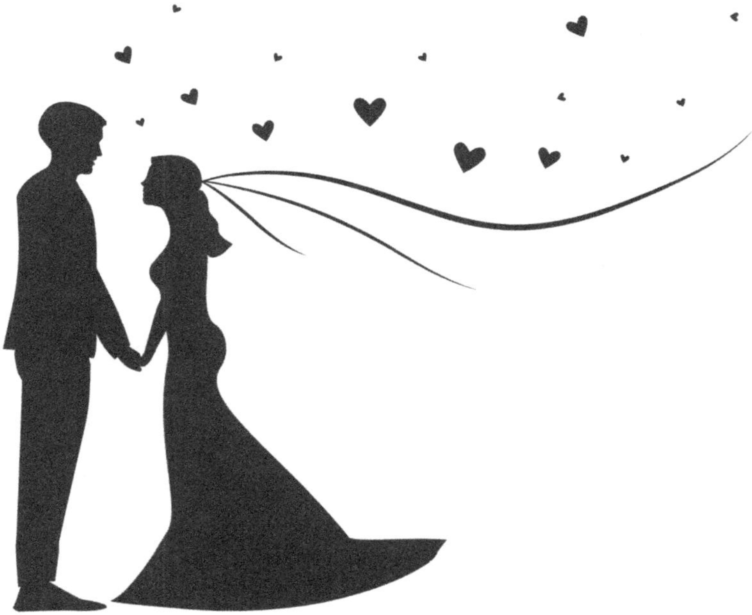

WHAT IS MY DAUGHTER-IN-LAW GOING TO CALL ME?

My mom asked me what my new daughter is going to call me.

I hadn't really thought about it.

Apparently back in the day what you called your mother-in-law was a thing. Like if you didn't call her "mom" it was a statement about your relationship.

I'm still traumatized by the fact that I'm a mother-in-law. Not because my son is married. He actually found the perfect human being; as I've said, they fit together like two puzzle pieces. And I'm not upset about being a mother-in-law because I don't love my new daughter; honestly there's nothing not to love there.

It's just that the title "mother-in-law" comes with a whole lot of connotations, none of which are positive. There are tons of movies and television shows about mothers-in-law. How they are overbearing and huge buttinskies and just plain awful.

In the movie "Monster-in-Law" Jane Fonda tries to break up her son (played by Michael Vartan) and his fiancée Charlie (played by the adorable and sweet Jennifer Lopez). Fonda's character Viola even nearly kills Charlie by getting her to eat something with nuts (Charlie is super allergic).

Hollywood has made a fortune off maligning mothers-in-law.

I have considered starting a movement to create a new title for being your new daughter or son's spouse's mother.

In any event, I'm not super hung up on what my new daughter calls me. In fact, I'm not super hung up on what anyone calls me. I am more concerned about what they say and how they feel than with how they summon my attention.

For example, my middle son had a very polite friend whose parents insisted that he use the formal titles "Mr." and "Mrs." when addressing adults. One day, when this little boy's playdate at my house was cut short because his mom wanted him home for dinner, he said to me, "This playdate sucked Mrs. F." I think you get my point here.

But just in case I was supposed to broach this subject, I did. I flat out asked my new daughter what she wanted to call me. And she said she thought she would continue to call me by my first name. Works for me. After all, she has a perfectly good mom of her own.

My only hope is that whatever she calls me, she does call me. Or texts me. Because I love hearing from her. And I hope that she likes me because that's a whole lot more important to me than how she addresses me.

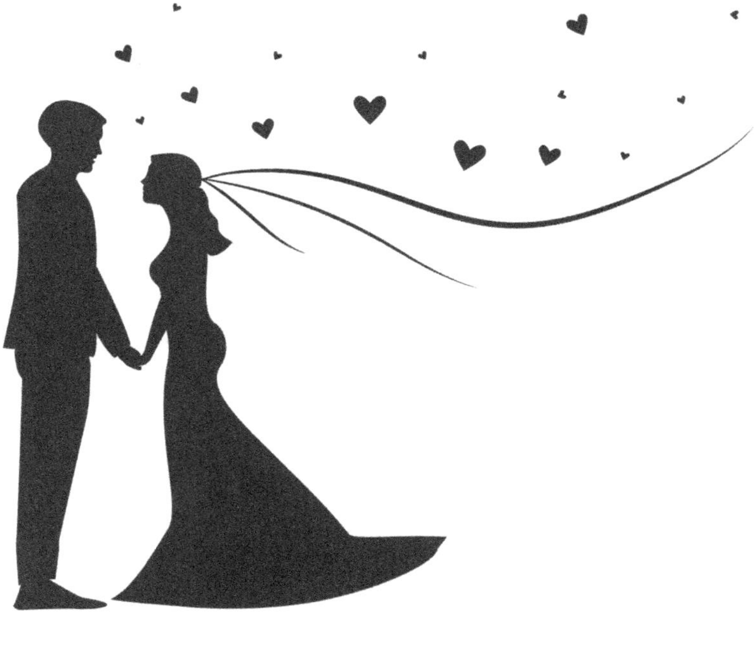

ADVICE TO THE NEWLYWEDS

*B*eing a writer, it was only a matter of time until I wrote something about how to live happily ever after.

The long and short of it is . . . I have no friggin' idea. If I did, I'd be rich and famous which, last time I checked, I'm not. I'm just a blogger from the burbs.

However (there's always a however in my posts), I have been married for 33 years and I do have a few thoughts on the subject.

For starters, marriage takes commitment. If you're not sure about entering into a LIFETIME situation, simply don't do it. Of course, you can get divorced, but that's just not an ideal way to think about it at the onset. From what I've seen, divorce can be messy and ugly, and everyone loses.

I think that my son and his fiancée have what it takes to go the distance. I see the way they look at each other, and even more importantly, the way they listen to each other.

Which leads me to my next point; listening and hearing. Everyone wants to be heard and validated and when you become a husband or a wife, you are signing on to be the person who listens. Even when you're bored and don't want to. The key is PRETENDING.

Sometimes I talk about handbags and I know my husband is dying of boredom. And sometimes he talks about work things or who got traded to what team and I cock my head to one side and nod so that he knows I'm at least trying. Trying is key.

It's also important to fight fairly. No bringing up old disputes. I mean, why bother dredging up the past when there's always so much new material? In addition, and this point helped me win a New York Times Modern Love contest where, not to brag, I beat out 10,000 other entries, NEVER BRING UP SIMILARITIES BETWEEN YOUR SPOUSE AND YOUR MOTHER-IN-LAW DURING A FIGHT. No good can come of saying "You sound just like your mother (or father)."

Compromise, compromise, compromise. Like if you want sushi and he wants Italian, have one on Monday and the other on Tuesday. Or if he wants to watch something violent and bloody and you want to watch a romantic comedy, watch a documentary on penguins. Because everyone loves penguins. You get my drift.

Of course, be faithful, both emotionally and physically. Maintain a sense of humor (you're really going to need one when your kids become teens), look up from your devices, remember to have fun, and always remember what made you fall in love in the first place.

No two marriages are the same and it's up to each couple to figure out what's right for them. Find your own path as a couple.

That rule about not going to sleep angry? It never worked for me and my husband. Sometimes we needed to stew a little longer before forgiving the other for whatever transgression occurred. But forgiveness is key—just remember no one is perfect and we all make mistakes. Try and learn from those mistakes, listen to (and actually hear) each other, and then move on.

Keep finding ways to surprise and delight one another through small gestures as well as grand acts. Putting each other person's needs first will increase your own happiness.

Remember to laugh. A lot. So much of life is absurdly funny—don't be more serious than you absolutely have to be.

I know there's more, a lot more. But that's a good start.

LOSING MY MIND

I've talked a lot about how I gained a daughter but less about how I nearly lost my mind. It's there, but kind of in-between the lines.

It wasn't just the wedding planning that threatened my sanity. When the pandemic started, my youngest son abruptly returned from his freshman year at college, finished his courses online and tried to make the most of things when his summer job as a counselor was nixed by the pandemic. My oldest son and almost daughter fled their apartment in Brooklyn, taking up residence first in my mom's nearby empty house and then at my mother-in-law's. When the grandmas came home from Florida, the kids moved in here. Through it all, my oldest son spent many days wandering room to room at my house working and on conference calls. My husband was working 15, 16-hour days, seven days a week. Middle son also moved back home from Manhattan, trying to find his own space in the house to work while his girlfriend, who was also with us, finished her senior year coursework online. Eventually, she went back home to Michigan and he was furloughed temporarily from his job. Between missing her and his job situation, middle son was corona cranky. We all were.

My empty nest had refilled really quickly. Those early days and weeks of the virus were especially scary. Here in New York, Covid-19 cases were out of control. I stopped going to the supermarket, which is like my second home, and spent hours online trying to procure a slot to get groceries delivered. And with everyone around we needed a lot of groceries. The food I had purchased before quarantine began and, which I thought would be enough for months, disappeared quickly. I had forgotten how much my sons can eat.

All of us were working from different rooms. When I tried to write or edit, I could barely hear myself think. I was terrified one of us would get sick; every time my throat felt scratchy or someone coughed, or even cleared their throat, I panicked.

We were trying to help our moms figure out how and when to get back safely from Florida and in time to quarantine before the wedding.

It was a lot, even without the stress of a wedding. Especially when you are an anxious person to begin with. And I am definitely an anxious person to begin with.

On the one hand, focusing on something other than Covid-19 or trying to find paper towels and toilet paper was good for me. The wedding was a pleasant distraction. Choosing flowers definitely beat listening to the news, which was all bad.

On the other hand, the kids' upcoming nuptials started making me a little nuts. It isn't every day you live with a couple right before they get married. Emotions were running high for each of us; I felt overworked and underappreciated.

My almost daughter worried about not getting her dress in time. (She got her gown only six days before the wedding.) I knew she missed her own family. My son became obsessed with the Phish cover band and where they would fit in our not so huge yard. (They ended up on our deck, which turned out to be a perfect stage.) At some point, I relinquished control to the bride and groom because, although the wedding was going to be at my house, it was their day. I got mad. They got mad. But we all got over it. Because that is what family does.

I am happy to say that I am as sane as I was before the events of spring/early summer. Which isn't saying all that much but it's something.

I NEARLY lost my mind. But I didn't.

WHO WILL PLAY ME IN THE MOTION PICTURE?

I have been thinking about who would play me when this book gets optioned to become a major motion picture.

Of course, my initial thought was that I would love to be portrayed by Meryl Streep. I mean, she's just so darn good. However, I feel that at 71, she might be a little too old to play me. Don't get me wrong, there are plenty of days when I FEEL like 71, but at 56 I don't think I look a day over 65. Plus, Meryl doesn't look enough like me to pull it off. Sorry Meryl.

Then a friend suggested Jennifer Garner. I mean, who doesn't love Jennifer Garner? She is just so wholesome and all-American. I still think Ben Affleck was an idiot to let her go. But not to sound like Goldilocks, Jennifer is a little too young to play me. Plus, I can't imagine her yelling at her kids with the same ferocity as I do. She's too nice. Scratch Jennifer.

In my heart of hearts, I feel like Sandra Bullock is the woman for the job. I loved her in a lot of her movies, but I thought she was especially good in "The Blind Side." Although she is one year younger than I am and way prettier, I feel like with some makeup she could look haggard enough to be me. And she would need to gain a few pounds. I could send her cookies. Plus, she does funny and vulnerable at the same time really well. Yup, it's got to be Sandy.

Since the book is about my son and new daughter's recent backyard wedding, we will need actors to play all of our family members as well. I feel strongly about my husband being played by George Clooney and he (my husband, not George) is totally on board. First of all, my husband and George are only four days apart in age. Plus, although my husband and I are married 33 years and I couldn't be happier, this is my chance to sort of be married to George. In addition, Sandy and George have been in a bunch of movies together and I feel like they have good chemistry.

I think my kids should have input as to who plays them, but I do have some ideas. Like my youngest son could be played by the actor who plays Adam Goldberg on "The Goldbergs." And my mother-in-law NEEDS to be played by Betty White because I totally adore Betty. She's a legend.

As the writer and consultant on the movie, I imagine that once the pandemic ends, I would fly out to Hollywood where I will be wined and dined. And the studio will put me up in a really nice hotel where I don't have to lift a finger for weeks. If the movie takes longer than expected to film, maybe they could rent me a house on the beach in Malibu.

They may want to film some of it on location here in my actual backyard which is fine. I don't think my neighbors would mind.

This movie is going to make the audience laugh and cry. In fact, it's going to be so good that it will likely be nominated for several Oscars. I think I'd like to wear Calvin Klein.

WRAPPING IT UP

We started out expecting to have a big wedding. We ended up with a micro wedding. It may have been small in numbers, but it was big in love.

Life is like that sometimes. Things don't happen as you expect. And then you have to figure out what to do next.

Living with your kids while planning a wedding in your backyard isn't as easy as I have made it sound. I don't want any of you to get the wrong impression. As I alluded to in an earlier chapter, there were fights and tears. And times when I was ready to run away from home to escape the chaos and insanity. But where would I have gone during a pandemic?

However, I now realize that there was beauty in the chaos. When I look at the pictures from that day, I see such joy and happiness. It was an event which surpassed our expectations. We've all said that we wish we could relive it. But I guess that's what the video and pictures are for.

My son and new daughter had originally thought that they might have another wedding in a year. Or at least a big party so that they could celebrate with friends and family.

But now they say they are done because they feel that this wedding was the real deal and satisfied them on every level. They are ready to move on. I had hoped that they would feel this way and I am so glad that they do.

Perhaps our story will inspire someone out there who is trying to figure out what to do about their own waylaid plans. A pandemic might dictate some things, but not everything.

In the end, how you proceed is entirely up to you.

Gained a Daughter But Nearly Lost My Mind

My Family

Bride's family

*Drone shot of celebration
(credit Greg Skriloff)*

ABOUT THE AUTHOR

Marlene Kern Fischer is a wife, mother of three grown sons and a recently gained new daughter, food shopper extraordinaire, blogger, lifelong writer and college essay editor. She attended Brandeis University, from which she graduated *cum laude* with a degree in English Literature. A Founding Contributor and Advisor for CollegiateParent, her work has also been featured in *The New York Times* (Modern Love), *The Huffington Post*, Kveller, the Erma Bombeck Writers' Workshop and Her View From Home. She is also a regular contributor for Grown and Flown. You can read some of Marlene's work on her Facebook page, *Thoughts From Aisle 4*.

CPSIA information can be obtained
at www.ICGtesting.com
Printed in the USA
LVHW082343161020
668889LV00010B/205